LeBron James

By Jeff Savage

Lerner Publications Company • Minneapolis

Lerner Publications Company
A division of Lerner Publishing Group, Inc.
241 First Avenue North
Minneapolis, Minnesota U.S.A.

Website address: www.lernerbooks.com

Library of Congress Cataloging-in-Publication Data

Savage, Jeff, 1961–
  LeBron James / by Jeff Savage.
      p.   cm.—(Amazing athletes)
    Includes index.
    ISBN-13: 978-0-8225-2947-7 (lib. bdg. : alk. paper)
    ISBN-10: 0-8225-2947-5 (lib. bdg. : alk. paper)
    1. James, LeBron—Juvenile literature. 2. Basketball players—United States—Biography—
  Juvenile literature. I. Title. II. Series.
  GV884.J36S38 2006
  796.72'092—dc22   2005011072

Manufactured in the United States of America
5 6 7 8 9 10 – DP – 13 12 11 10 09 08

TABLE OF CONTENTS

LeBron shoots over Brad Miller of the Sacramento Kings.

A Super Start

LeBron James jumped high in the air and let the basketball fly. It sailed to the basket and ripped through the net. Swish! LeBron had just made his first basket in the pros!

Moments later, he sank a **fadeaway jump shot.** Then he made a **steal** and soared toward the basket. LeBron slammed down a thunderous **dunk** and ran back down the court flashing his million-dollar smile.

LeBron jumps high in the air and slams the ball through the hoop.

More than 17,000 fans had filled Arco Arena in Sacramento, California. They were there to see how LeBron and his Cleveland Cavaliers would do against the hometown Sacramento Kings. Millions of viewers were watching the game on television.

LeBron was just an 18-year-old kid playing in his first game in the National Basketball Association (NBA). LeBron had gone straight from high school to the pros. Only 1 in 10,000 high school players ever makes it to the pro level. Few have the skill and talent to skip college. Most who go straight to the pros don't play much at first. They have to learn a lot before they are ready to play against the very best.

LeBron and Doug Christie of the Kings chase after a loose ball.

LeBron dribbles around Kings player Mike Bibby.

But LeBron was already playing like a wise **veteran.** He quickly showed that he was the best player on the Cavaliers team. He scored 12 points in just the first quarter. He sprinted to the basket with a speedy dribble. Later, he dropped in a tough scoop shot. He also showed that he can help his teammates score. He made a brilliant high pass to teammate

Darius Miles. Miles leaped in the air and slammed the ball through the hoop. LeBron's great pass earned him an **assist.**

In the end, the Kings were the better team. The Cavaliers lost the game, 106–92. But LeBron showed why his nickname is King James. He finished with 25 points, 9 assists, 6 **rebounds,** and 4 steals.

"Playing with NBA players was a dream come true," LeBron said afterward. "I'm afraid to pinch myself because I might wake up."

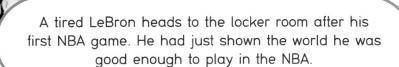

A tired LeBron heads to the locker room after his first NBA game. He had just shown the world he was good enough to play in the NBA.

LeBron grew up in Akron, Ohio.

ON THE MOVE

LeBron James was born December 30, 1984, in Akron, Ohio. He lived with his mother, Gloria. LeBron never met his father. "My mother is my everything," LeBron says.

Gloria and LeBron were very poor. They lived in a troubled part of town. At the age of five,

LeBron and his mother moved seven times. Once they lived in an apartment building that was so run-down the city had it closed and torn down. "I saw drugs, guns, killings," said LeBron. "It was crazy. But my mom kept food in my mouth and clothes on my back."

Gloria's boyfriend was a man named Eddie Jackson. LeBron called him Dad. Sometimes Jackson lived with LeBron and his mother. Other times, Jackson did not.

LeBron with his mom (right) and Eddie Jackson.

LeBron's unsettled home life made school hard for him. He missed 82 days of school in fourth grade. So Gloria sent LeBron to live with his youth basketball coach, Frankie Walker. "It changed my life," said LeBron. In fifth grade, LeBron had perfect attendance and a B average. For the next few years, LeBron sometimes lived with Walker and other times with his mother.

LeBron loved playing sports. His favorite game was basketball. LeBron was a super player, even as a kid. In eighth grade, he led his school team to the finals of a national **tournament.** That same year, he threw down his first slam dunk. When he entered high school in 1999, LeBron was already over six feet tall.

LeBron's amazing basketball skills made him one of the best high school players in the country.

SOARING HIGH

LeBron was a star at Saint Vincent-Saint Mary (SVSM) High School. As a **freshman,** or first-year student, he led the SVSM Irish to the Ohio state championship. He did it again in his **sophomore** year.

LeBron and his teammates celebrate winning the Ohio state championship during LeBron's freshman year.

That season, he was named Ohio's Mr. Basketball. This meant he was the top high school player in the state. He was the first sophomore to earn the title.

By his **junior** year, LeBron stood 6 feet 7 inches tall. He was fast and very strong. He could jump incredibly high. Other high school players didn't stand a chance against him. Meanwhile, NBA **scouts** had been watching LeBron. "He's the best high school player I've ever seen," said one scout.

LeBron's skills made him famous. Thousands of people wanted to see him play. The SVSM gym didn't have enough seats to hold all the fans! So the Irish played its home games at the nearby University of Akron.

Tickets for LeBron's games sold for as high as $20. About 4,000 people showed up for each game. Even NBA superstars like Shaquille O'Neal came to see King James play. Los Angeles Lakers star Kobe Bryant gave LeBron a special pair of shoes with U.S. flags on them.

Shaquille O'Neal was one of several NBA players who came to see LeBron play at the University of Akron.

LeBron takes the ball to the hoop during his junior year in high school.

LeBron didn't let his fans down. In one game against the best team in the country, he scored an amazing 36 points. At the end of the season, scouts agreed that LeBron was already good enough to play in the NBA. They said that LeBron would be the first pick in the **draft** if he left high school a year early. "That is not going to happen," LeBron said. "I can do more to get my brain and my game ready if I finish school."

LeBron reads an article about himself in *Sports Illustrated* magazine. LeBron was famous around the country by his **senior** year in high school.

HITTING THE BIG TIME

LeBron was just 17 when he started his senior year in high school in 2002. But it was hard for him to stay a kid. He was the most popular high school basketball player ever. He appeared on the cover of *Sports Illustrated* magazine. TV camera crews followed him to school every day.

But LeBron didn't let all the attention drive him crazy. He tried to live a normal life. He went to movies with his friends. He played games on his Sony PlayStation 2. He ate huge bowls of Fruity Pebbles and Cinnamon Toast Crunch for breakfast—and dinner. He even made sure to keep his bedroom clean!

LeBron also worked on his game. He shot nearly 800 jump shots every day. Most important, he earned good grades. "He knows schoolwork comes first," said his mother. "No work, no basketball."

LeBron has a little fun while sitting at his locker.

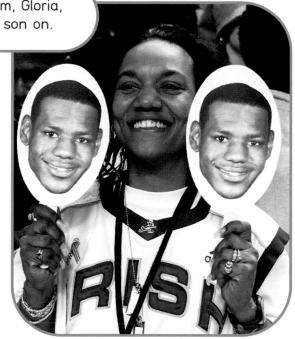

LeBron's mom, Gloria, cheers her son on.

By LeBron's senior year, ESPN was showing his games on TV. In one game, LeBron scored 31 points and grabbed 13 rebounds to beat the best high school team in the country.

LeBron usually scored more than 30 points a game that year. Coach Dru Joyce said his star could have scored 50. But LeBron's favorite play has always been making a great pass. "I love sharing the ball with my teammates," he says. At the end of the season, LeBron's Irish were ranked first in the nation by *USA Today*.

LeBron shakes hands with NBA commissioner David Stern. LeBron was the first player taken in the 2003 NBA Draft.

Soon after, LeBron signed a **contract** with the Nike sports equipment company. He agreed to make ads for Nike for seven years. In return, they would pay him $90 million! LeBron was suddenly rich beyond his wildest dreams.

LeBron finished high school in the spring of 2003. In June, LeBron and his mom attended the 2003 NBA Draft. NBA commissioner David Stern walked on stage to announce the first pick. "With the first pick of the 2003 NBA Draft, the Cleveland Cavaliers select LeBron James."

LeBron walked up on stage in his fancy white suit. He smiled and shook hands with the commissioner. LeBron had become a pro. His dream had come true.

But the Cavaliers were a losing team. In 2002, they had the worst record in basketball. Cavaliers fans hoped LeBron could turn things around. But he was just 18 years old. Was he good enough to be a star in the best basketball league in the world? "There's a lot of pressure on me," he said, "but I don't put a lot of pressure on myself."

LeBron holds up his new Cleveland Cavaliers jersey. LeBron wears number 23 in honor of his favorite basketball player, Michael Jordan.

LeBron dribbles the ball around Bruce Bowen of the San Antonio Spurs.

INSTANT SUPERSTAR

LeBron made the Cavaliers a hot ticket. Fans across the country wanted to see the young **rookie** play. Arenas filled up with fans for all of LeBron's games. And thousands of fans bought copies of LeBron's number 23 jersey. It became the top-selling NBA jersey.

But was LeBron a good enough player to live up to the excitement? He soon showed that he was. After his big night in Sacramento, he scored 21 points against the Phoenix Suns. Then he scored 23 against the Indiana Pacers. But LeBron alone wasn't enough to make the Cavs winners. The team lost their first five games.

Finally, LeBron led his team to wins over the Washington Wizards and New York Knicks. Then the Cavs lost eight games in a row. In one of those games, LeBron scored 33 points, grabbed 16 rebounds, and added 7 assists.

LeBron is friends with Cincinnati Reds slugger Ken Griffey Jr. LeBron met Junior at a Cleveland Indians game. LeBron even got to take batting practice!

LeBron hangs on the rim after a monster dunk at the 2004 Olympic Games in Athens, Greece. The U.S. Olympic Basketball Team finished in third place.

In the end, the Cavaliers did not make the **playoffs.** Still, LeBron was among the top 15 players in the NBA in scoring, steals, and assists. It was a great season for such a young player.

In the summer of 2004, LeBron was invited to play on the U.S. Basketball Team at the 2004 **Summer Olympic Games.** He played alongside superstars Tim Duncan, Amare Stoudamire, and Carmelo Anthony. At the Olympic Games in Athens, Greece, the team finished in third place. Each player was awarded a **bronze medal.**

LeBron jumps high to slam the ball through the hoop during his second NBA season.

LeBron started his next season ready to take the Cavs to the playoffs. He led his team to a strong record in the first half of the season. LeBron continued to impress everyone with his great play.

"It's weird talking about a 20-year old kid being a great player," said one NBA coach. "But he is a great player, and he could be the best ever."

In late December 2004, LeBron was hurt in a game. Dikembe Mutombo of the Houston Rockets accidentally elbowed LeBron in the face. LeBron's cheekbone was broken. He had to wear a special mask to protect his face.

Still, LeBron kept up his great play. He shined in his first **NBA All-Star Game.** He had made 13 points, 8 assists, and 6 rebounds. But as the season went on, the Cavs played badly. During one stretch, the team lost 9 of 12 games.

Wearing a special face mask allowed LeBron to play with a broken cheekbone.

LeBron goes up for a rebound against Phoenix Suns player Shawn Marion at the 2005 NBA All-Star Game.

That season, LeBron played more minutes and scored more baskets than any other player in the NBA. His **scoring average** was just over 27 points per game. This was third best in the NBA. He also was third in steals and finished among the top 10 in many other categories. Still, the Cavaliers missed the 2005 playoffs. They had a winning record, but they fell one win short.

LeBron continues to work hard to be the best. But he also takes some time to relax and have some fun.

LeBron set his sights higher. He worked harder to improve. "If you are not pushing yourself or no one is pushing you, you will not get better," LeBron explains. "That is true in sports and school."

Selected Career Highlights

2006–2007   Led all players in votes for the NBA All-Star Game

2005–2006   Ranked second in league in scoring and second in total
minutes played
Named Most Valuable Player of the NBA All-Star Game

2004–2005   Played more minutes than any other NBA player
Ranked third in league in scoring, third in steals, sixth in
assists
Scored 13 points in his first NBA All-Star Game
Won a bronze medal as a member of 2004 U.S. Olympic
Basketball Team

2003–2004   Named NBA Rookie of the Year
Became the third NBA rookie to average 20 points,
5 rebounds, and 5 assists per game
Led all rookies in steals and was ranked second
in scoring
Named Eastern Conference Rookie of the
Month every month of the season
First player taken in the 2003 NBA Draft

2002–2003   Named Mr. Basketball in Ohio for the
third time
Named Parade Player of
the Year for the second
time
Named National Player
of the Year

2001–2002   Named Mr. Basketball in
Ohio for the second time
Named Parade Player
of the Year

2000–2001   First sophomore ever named
Mr. Basketball in Ohio

Glossary

assist: a pass to a teammate that helps that teammate score a basket

bronze medal: at the Olympics, a medal awarded to a third-place finisher

contract: a written deal agreed to and signed by a player and a team or a company

draft: a yearly event in which professional sports teams take turns choosing new players from a selected group

dunk: slamming the basketball through the hoop

fadeaway jump shot: a shot in which the shooter jumps and shoots the ball while falling away from the basket

freshman: first-year student

junior: third-year student

NBA All-Star Game: a midseason game in which the best players in the league play

playoffs: a series of games to decide the league's champion

rebounds: grabbing missed shots

rookie: a first-year player

scoring average: a number that describes how many points a player scores per game. The NBA's best players usually score more than 20 points per game.

scouts: people hired by teams to look for their future players

senior: fourth-year student

sophomore: second-year student

steal: taking the ball from the other team's player

Summer Olympic Games: an event held every four years in which athletes from around the world compete in dozens of different sports

tournament: a set of games held to decide the best team

veteran: a player who has played several years

Further Reading & Websites

Jones, Ryan. *King James: Believe the Hype, the LeBron James Story*. New York: St. Martin's Griffin, 2003.

Mattern, Joanne. *LeBron James*. Hockessin, DE: Mitchell Lane Publishers, 2005.

Morgan Jr., David Lee. *LeBron James: The Rise of a Star*. Cleveland: Gray & Co., 2003.

Cleveland Cavaliers Website
http://www.nba.com/cavaliers
The official website of the Cavaliers includes team schedules, news, profiles of past and present players and coaches, and much more.

LeBron James: The Official Website
http://www.lebronjames.com
LeBron's official website features news, statistics, trivia, photos, and a diary from LeBron.

NBA Website
http://www.nba.com
The NBA's official website provides fans with recent news stories, statistics, biographies of players and coaches, and information about games.

Sports Illustrated for Kids
http://www.sikids.com
The *Sports Illustrated for Kids* website covers all sports, including basketball.

Index

Photo Acknowledgments

Photographs are used with the permission of: © Mike Blake/Reuters/CORBIS, pp. 4, 6, 7, 8, 9; © Jim Baron/The Image Finders, p. 10; © Copyright. Akron Beacon. All rights reserved. Distributed by Valeo IP., pp. 11, 14, 17; © Bob Falcetti/Icon SMI, p. 13; © Jim Redman/Icon SMI, p. 15; © Michael J. LeBrecht II/NewSport/CORBIS, pp. 16, 18; AP/Wide World Photos, pp. 19, 20, 21; © William Luther/San Antonio Express-News/ZUMA Press, p. 22; © A Bibard/Fep/Panoramic/ZUMA Press, p. 24; © Icon Sports Media, p. 25; © Bob Leverone/SportingNews/ZUMA Press, p. 26; © John Gress/Icon SMI, p. 27; © Gary Caskey/Reuters/CORBIS, p. 28; © Hyungwon Kang/Reuters/CORBIS, p. 29.

Front cover: © John Gress/Icon SMI.